Praise fo

"Justin Zufelt uses his own struggles and the vast experience he has gained to lead others out of Satan's 'kill zone' by outlining clear steps to overcoming temptations. If young and old readers alike take this book to heart and follow the steps with true sincerity, then Satan will surely lose all hold over their hearts and minds."

-Seth, age 19

"This book made a great comparison between how warfare has changed over the centuries and how Satan has changed his attacks on us as well. This perspective helps us to be aware and to have a stronger foundation so we can defend ourselves and our families."

-Caleb, age 15

"This was a great book! The author's life experience and the scripture stories really connected everything together and made a difficult topic interesting and easier to understand. I loved the thought questions at the end of each chapter! They helped me to really think about what I had read and how it related to my life."

-Courtney, age 13

"I really liked this book a lot. I really liked that it was interesting to read. It has a lot of cool stories which made it intriguing. It was

helpful for me to read about how dangerous pornography is and how it has affected so many people's lives. It was neat to see a different perspective on the scripture stories that I know and how they can help us understand addiction better. This book also talks a lot about Satan's power to tempt us to do a lot of things that are wrong. It wasn't just about pornography, but all kinds of temptations, sins, and weaknesses and how they can affect our lives."

-Rebecca, age 12

"This is a very interesting book! It phrases things in a way that makes sense and is easy to understand. Though it is easy to understand, it also makes you think and reassess yourself and your choices. I also like that it is nondenominational. Overall, it's a great book and I would recommend it to all my friends."

-Elisabeth, age 16

"The Kill Zone *gave me powerful mental tools that I will use for the rest of my life. It uses biblical stories as examples of why addictions are so harmful and how to overcome them. I think that because of the way the book is written, it will appeal to other kids my age.*"

-Calem, age 12

"The Kill Zone *gave me specific examples of people who have overcome addictions and how they did it. It's good to see how real people overcame their problems. It is a well-written book that is easy to digest."*

-Heaton, age 14

"I have been really inspired by this book. All of the stories and applying the lessons taught by them to yourself really makes a difference. I highly recommend people who are just starting to go through trials mentioned in this book read it soon and share it with others that you know are going through the same types of trials. Some of the things mentioned in this book have never even crossed my mind. This book is very captivating; I read to page 90 without putting it down. Please read this book and don't give up hope. This book is going to show all the tools that you have and how to use them and you will be successful."

-Aaron, age 15

"This book is great for all teens of any age; it teaches many great and valuable lessons through examples, stories, and analogies that are incredibly relatable and have powerful meanings. This book introduces tips and ideas for staying out of or getting out of what Zufelt calls 'the kill zone.' It encourages teens to stay strong against temptation and helps them learn how to recognize it before it's too late."

-Kayla, age 17

"I appreciate this book. It has some unique and interesting perspectives on pornography avoidance that are invaluable to

understand, such as the concepts of the Delilah Cycle and the Flash Bang Technique that are certainly some of Satan's biggest tools. I think this book is worth the read. And worth it more than once."

-Rachel, age 21

"Reading this book opened my eyes to the reality of the struggles of teenage life. Learning about the kill zone and tools to stay away from it are very valuable and something that can be very useful and helpful to every teenager."

-Gracie, age 16

"I would definitely recommend this book to any of my friends. The author uses real life situations that all teens can relate to. This book was very skillfully written."

-Hallee, age 13

"This is an amazing book that teaches teens how to resist temptation and stay out of the kill zone before we're even put in it. It helps us train our minds to be prepared for any kind of temptation Satan throws at us, and because we already know how to deal with temptation, we can get out of the kill zone very quickly and mostly unharmed. This is a book that is helpful for anyone who's going through a trial, someone who's wanting to better themselves, or someone that just wants to learn a little bit."

-AnnaLeah, age 15

Discover Your Strength | Achieve Your Purpose

Mission Statement

Operation Onward Miracle is helping youth discover their inner spiritual strength, overcome a world plagued by pornography, and realize the miracle that is in them to achieve their God-given purpose. We do this by educating, inspiring, and providing the tools needed for success.

www.operationonwardmiracle.com

THE KILL ZONE

A Spiritual Survival Guide for
Combating Pornography and Other
Addictions

Justin Zufelt

Copyright © 2019 Operation Onward Miracle
All rights reserved.

No part of this book may be reproduced in any form or by any electronic or mechanical means, including information storage and retrieval systems, without permission in writing from the publisher.

Published by Operation Onward Miracle
Printed in the United States of America

Cover Design: Terri Zora

ISBN-13: 978-1-7326035-9-2
ISBN-10: 1-7326035-9-6

Library of Congress Control Number: 2019936542

To God.

And to the youth who are called to carry on the battle.

TABLE OF CONTENTS

Introduction	1
Mellow Yellow	3
Spiritual Kill Zone	11
The Delilah Cycle	22
Flash Bang	30
Battlefields	34
Stay Alert, Stay Alive!	40
Ace	47
Battle Armor	63
Ultimate Warrior	73
Your Source of Power	79
God's Zone of Light	82
Conclusion	88
Suggested Action Steps	89
Songs	90
Bibliography	95

INTRODUCTION

I am grateful for the opportunity to share the reality of the Kill Zone with you. I will explain what this is later in the book, but just know for now that it is a true principle that can protect you just as it has protected men and women throughout history. When violated, however, it can bring down the mightiest leaders and those who follow them. This book was written with your success in mind and will help you identify your power, abilities, and gifts for victory.

I know you can be victorious!

Throughout my life and career in the military and law enforcement, I have been given specific trials, training, and experiences that can benefit you in your journey through life. These tools and insights, when applied, can be used to win your personal battles and ultimately win your war. In fact, one of the most important lessons I'm going to teach you is the reality that you do NOT have to fight many of the battles that will arise in your life! At times you will find yourself at a point where a simple choice will either lead you down the path toward safety or the path toward hardship. By the end of the book, I hope you see this truth, learn the principles, and find strength to develop the skills needed to survive the Kill Zone!

Let us begin!

MELLOW YELLOW

Y ou never forget the first door you kick in! I remember every detail of the mellow yellow-colored, single-wide trailer, which sat as the third trailer to the left on the third row of a local trailer park. It was just after 2 p.m. on a warm June day. The combination of heat, gear, and excitement was leading me to sweat profusely. We parked our cars and walked into the trailer park quickly and quietly.

It was my first year on the police force, and a call had come in that the drug task force was requesting an immediate response from any available police officers. We were informed that children were in danger, a no-knock search warrant had been granted, and entry had to be made quickly! A plan was thrown together, and we put it into action. I was the first on scene, which made me the number one man (first to enter the home after kicking the door open), or so the other officers told me.

There I was, standing on top of some rickety wood steps in front of six other officers. Four of the officers were uniformed while the two at the back were plainclothes drug task force officers. The two task force officers didn't stay in the stick (line); instead, they walked around trying to get a good view of the back of the trailer. They wanted to see if anyone was running away.

I felt the squeeze on my shoulder signaling that those behind me were ready to go. I stepped to the left to give myself ample kicking room for maximum effect. I raised my foot up and aimed for the sweet spot—slightly left and down from the door knob.

Any situation that forces you to be channeled through a small area and causes a group of soldiers or law enforcement officers to slow down and bunch together is called a Fatal Funnel, Vortex of Death, or more commonly, the Kill Zone. It is an area that both good guys *and* bad guys know about. For one side to get to the other, the area must be crossed. This makes it a lot easier for the defending side to harm anyone coming through. You can focus your weapons at the funneled area with a higher probability of killing those you're aiming at. The Kill Zone.

With the motivation welling up in me to not be on the unstable stairs a second longer than necessary, I gave the door one swift punt and the door disappeared! To me, the door must have exploded with my raw, awesome power, but I came to find out the owners had used a single-walled interior closet door for the front door. In other words, it was a very weak door. In slow motion, I watched wood splinters fling through the air like confetti in a New Year's Eve celebration.

I remember walking through the doorway and feeling like life was moving in slow motion. I walked in like I owned the place, slow and cocky! Not a thought of fear, or even the mission, passed through my head. All I could think about was how euphoric my first entry into a home was! I couldn't believe the intoxicating adrenaline high!

The six other officers were not as excited—or dimwitted—as I. They quickly went through the home looking for the suspects. I strolled around giving thumbs up and mouthing, "Did you see that?!" The other officers responded with an exaggerated eye roll as they pushed past to work.

Luckily for me, no one was home. Had there been a confrontation at the door, I would have been toast! In no way was I ready for a fight. I was blind to all but my own superiority. Countless men and women have lost their lives making entries into homes. I was blessed that day to keep my life.

Afterward, I had an incredible team around me that took their time to teach me how to quickly get through the Kill Zone. They taught me that the worst thing I could ever do was to stop or move slowly through the doorway. They explained that every second spent in the doorway doubled the chance of being harmed or killed. It took years of training and experience to develop the skills needed to survive, and even then, I had to continue practicing and learning daily to keep them sharp and reflexive. Like all knowledge, survival skills are perishable!

History of the Kill Zone

Have you ever seen a battle scene from a Robin Hood-era movie? Take a second and think back to the movies you have watched. Do you remember the scenes in which two opposing armies stand on a field facing each other? Can you see the heavy early morning mist coming from the horses' nostrils and the knights in their glimmering armor holding their swords, spears, and banners? As the camera pans around the battlefield, you are shown the archers and catapults in the distance.

Now start the battle with me. The heroic leader rides forward and offers his epic speech. After much cheering and grandstanding, a signal of either a sound or banner waving in the distance notifies everyone that the battle is about to commence. The two sides usually begin to advance toward each other. As the horses and footmen gradually increase their speed for the impending collision with the opposing force, we break away from the battlefield to a safe position behind the lines.

Here stand the archers and catapults. They are a safe distance from the opposing force; nevertheless, they stand ready to inflict mass casualties on their foes. Watch as the archers draw their arrows from their quivers in unison. They take the command to notch their arrows, draw back, hold, and then release! We see hundreds or even thousands of arrows soaring through the air. The arrows fly high into the sky and then come raining down on the opposing army.

This scene was played out for thousands of years by countless societies. It shows that the enemy knows the battlefield and uses very specific tactics against the opposing force.

Next, consider the strategy of the 1600-1700's. In this era, we saw a major shift from archers, catapults, and swords to muskets and cannons. The soldiers standing in mass formations along the battlefield stayed relatively similar. The main difference was the distance from the enemy. As weaponry became more lethal, the enemies stood farther apart. The soldiers packed close together, walked in lines, and shot at each other.

In the early 1900's, the tactic of standing shoulder to shoulder in mass formations waiting to be shot had all but vanished. Instead, soldiers would trench, berm, flank, and charge. With the increased use and development of machines, repeating rifles, rudimentary machine guns, larger bullets, and cannons, new methods had to be developed. But the tactics were still carried out on the open battlefield.

By World War II, we moved from trench warfare to tanks, planes, ships, submarines, beaches, air warfare, and the creation of squad tactics. The Kill Zone changed and covered the entire world. Roadways, canyons, water passages, hedges, and every other terrain feature became a source of funneling the enemy. Urban warfare also developed as a major part of fighting during this timeframe. Buildings and doorways became a prime location to create Kill Zones.

Now consider our recent warfare. The battlefield has shrunk to the most personal and accurate form known to man. A concrete dumb bomb can be aimed at your head—or your toe—and not miss. Just imagine what we can do with fully weaponized smart bombs. The creation of nanotechnology, drones, lasers, and radiation weapons can attack an individual right down to their atoms and nervous systems.

The newest battlefield is fought with cyber warfare. The tactic of funneling has been translated to the digital world. Cyber warriors find sources of weakness and attack areas where mass information is collected, changed, or destroyed.

European countries are proposing legislation to the United Nations to ban killer robots from being created.[1] These robots are designed to decide when to kill or not kill based on artificial intelligence. The robot will make these decisions with no human input. The decisions will be based on your personal life choices such as social media, library book lists, web searches, associations, etc.

War today is up close and personal. Each method described is specifically crafted and designed for an individual person. Gone are the days of carpet bombing and indiscriminate killing. It is specific, it is personal, and it is lethality to the max!

Now you understand that the Kill Zone model of warfare has been used in every war throughout the world's history. But the physical battlefield of some foreign war is not the only place it is used.

It is also the #1 tactic used by Satan on the spiritual battlefield!

Practical Exercise

1. How has Satan been attacking you on a personal level?

2. What issues did your grandparents have to face? How are they similar to the issues you are facing today?

3. What does the Kill Zone on the battlefield represent to you?

SPIRITUAL KILL ZONE

"For the wages of sin is death; but the gift of God is eternal life through Jesus Christ our Lord." -Romans 6:23

A spiritual Kill Zone follows the same structure as a physical Kill Zone. Instead of a doorway or grassy field, it happens in the battlefield of thought. If you are in the Kill Zone, then you are allowing your mind to remain focused on whatever Satan places there. Satan knows that the longer he keeps your mind occupied, the more vulnerable you become to sin and temptation. Every second you spend pondering on such things increases the potential of your soul and spirit being harmed!

During my study of the scriptures, I was introduced to incredible leaders who fell after their rise to power. I was amazed that so many leaders of the past kept falling for simple things, and I wanted to know why it happened. I dug into the scriptures deeper and spoke with experts to find the answer. After months of study, the foundation of the Kill Zone was built. It is the common thread that links each of the stories together.

I know that God inspired the authors of the Bible to write down specific accounts of physical challenges which directly correlate to spiritual matters. He is aware of the link and how powerful it is!

Here are a few stories from the Bible that teach us what to look for and how to defeat Satan's tactic.

Adam and Eve

There stood Adam and Eve in the Garden of Eden. They had been given dominion over the garden and all that was within. They were given specific instructions on what they should do and only one commandment of what not to do. Then the Father of Lies entered the picture and had to decide how to bring down our first parents. Where did he focus his time and efforts? Tempting Adam and Eve to send inappropriate texts or do drugs was a fruitless effort. (Do you see what I did there?)

Instead, he focused his time on tempting them with the forbidden fruit. Satan knew that this was a viable temptation if he could just get Adam and Eve to keep thinking about it. Satan spoke to our first parents quietly with appealing suggestions and temptations. That tactic was a success with Adam and Eve. Satan convinced Eve to eat the forbidden fruit, and she convinced Adam to do the same. Of course, God being God knew this would happen. Eve's actions led to the fulfilment of God's commandment to multiply and replenish the earth. Only when they were forced to leave the garden were they able to start a family.

Cain and Abel

This brings us to Cain and Abel. In Genesis 4:5 we read that Cain became "wroth" and his "countenance fell" after he and his brother, Abel, offered sacrifices to God. Cain's offering was refused while Abel's found favor with God. The phrase "his countenance fell" is what we are going to focus on. Why did it fall, and why did it stay fallen even after God discussed the issue with him? The reason is simple: Cain allowed his mind to linger on the refused sacrifice, which then allowed Satan to finally convince him to kill Abel. He remained in the Kill Zone when he allowed the emotions of pride, jealousy, and anger to fester in his mind, leading to the rationalization of murder.

King David

Another powerful example of the dangers of remaining in the Kill Zone is the story of King David. As a young boy and shepherd, David delivered supplies to his older brothers on the battlefront. Young David found the Israelite army at a standstill due to a lack of faith in God's protection. The Philistines challenged Israel to offer their greatest warrior to fight the Philistines' greatest warrior. The losing side must become slaves to the other. Showing great courage and faith, David entered the battlefield with a sling, slayed Goliath, and saved Israel from servitude.

Interesting side note: Did David go to the battlefield and have a fair fight with Goliath? Definitely not! He stood at a distance and slung a rock, which struck Goliath in the forehead and ended the fight. That is staying out of the Kill Zone at its finest!

Over time, David became the King of Israel and truly had everything. He had a kingdom, riches, good health, armies, and more wives and children than he could count. Most importantly, he held God's favor.

But one night while hanging out on his roof, he observed his neighbor, Bathsheba, bathing at her home. With what we know about the battlefield, we could definitely call this a Kill Zone moment in his life. He had two choices. The safe choice would be to quickly turn around and get out of the Kill Zone, remembering to never be on the rooftop at that time of day again. Instead of doing that, he chose to stay and watch. Now, I am making an educated guess, but I suspect King David watched her several times as he awaited word on who she was. Given the following choices that he made, it can be assumed that he took note of the time he saw her and ensured he returned at the same time and place in the future. He did what he could in hopes of seeing her again in the same vulnerable situation.

This would be like us accidentally viewing websites, videos, or movies that are inappropriate and then repeatedly returning. When David first saw Bathsheba and realized what was happening, he had not sinned. However, if he were to remain or return, then it would become an intentional act and a sin.

What did King David do?

He remained and watched Bathsheba and then sent his servants to inquire on her identity. Soon word came that Bathsheba was a married woman, and her husband, Uriah, was away fighting one of King David's wars. David made his decision by remaining in the Kill Zone and allowing Satan to tempt him with all manner of thoughts, the most dangerous being that of entitlement. David was convinced that whatever he wanted could be his due to his position. He remained in the Kill Zone, resulting in his stealing a man's wife, having a baby out of wedlock, and murdering an innocent man. Over 70,000 of his soldiers died, many of his own children were murdered, and worst of all, he lost favor with God. Talk about the consequences of remaining in the Kill Zone!

What do we learn here? Once David allowed himself to remain in the Kill Zone of temptation, Satan had ample time to convince him to act on his feelings. No matter how strong we think we are, we cannot remain in the Kill Zone unscathed. The Master of Lies has convinced the greatest warriors, kings, and prophets to sin. If we remain, he will convince us to act on what we are seeing, feeling, and thinking.

When David was done sinning, he sent Bathsheba home in secrecy. Like many sins, the consequences were slow to follow. After a couple of months, King David was notified by Bathsheba that she was pregnant. Did King David confess and deal with the sin correctly? Nope. Instead, he went to great lengths to hide his sin. First, he called Bathsheba's husband, Uriah, home from war. David did his best to put things in motion so that Uriah would have a reason to believe the baby was his own. David even went as far as getting Uriah drunk! But Uriah was an honorable man and believed that he should not have sexual gratification while his men were on the battlefield away from their wives. When David's feeble attempts failed, he sent Uriah back to the frontline of battle with the express direction to the commanders that he be placed in harm's way to ensure his death.

Think about it! This is King David, the man who was selected to be king as a young boy, the man who showed incredible faith in God as he faced Goliath, the man who showed patience and love when his father-in-law attempted to kill him on several occasions. Why would he do this? Why would he allow himself to go SO FAR DOWN?!

Practical Exercise

Similar Kill Zones that you may encounter are:

1. While searching online, you come across a website with inappropriate images.
2. You are watching a movie, and words, images, language, and/or actions are not up to the standards of a disciple of Christ.
3. You are attending a party where the music changes, dancing becomes inappropriate, and/or mind-altering substances are being shared around the room.

One or all of these examples will happen to you at some point. Take a moment and write down exactly how you will respond to each situation listed above.

1.

2.

3.

Walk Toward the Light

Each situation of temptation presents an opportunity for you to test Heavenly Father's promise that if we keep ourselves out of the Kill Zone, he will not allow us to be tempted above our abilities. Have faith in this promise. The most important thing you can do is be vocal about the temptation. Speak with your parents, religious leaders, and friends. Seek advice, mentorship, and support to help you through the situation. The more you sound the warning horn, the more support you will get!

Once Satan has convinced you to sin, he will then place shame and disgust in your heart. He will do everything he can to convince you to keep it hidden in the dark. The reason for this is simple and can be easily explained with one question: **Who rules the light, and who lingers in the darkness?** Satan wants to keep you in the dark where he is most powerful. As David lied and hid his sin, he was guided down the road of pain and misery.

On the bright side of this story, the tale ends with King David dying in God's good graces. He had a son with Bathsheba who was named Solomon and became one of the greatest kings of all time. That is, until his eventual fall due to his willingness to remain in the Kill Zone of pride!

Samson

Next, let us discuss another popular childhood story: Samson. Samson is another devastating example of one who remained in the Kill Zone. Samson was blessed with physical strength if he did not cut his hair. This blessing of strength and protection was proven time after time in battle. With this blessing, Samson became a scourge to the Philistines who could not defeat him. Samson was able to kill them with weapons, his bare hands, and even a jaw bone!

Then Samson met a beautiful woman named Delilah. He became infatuated with Delilah to the point where he allowed himself to be tempted by her and her desire to know the source of his strength. Delilah had made a deal with the Philistines to find the secret to Samson's strength. To be fair, we don't know why Delilah made the deal to betray Samson. It may have been for money, power, love, or protecting her family from the Philistines - we don't know. It's important not to judge her actions, just as we don't want others to judge us when they don't understand our situation. Whatever the reason, Delilah demanded that Samson prove his love to her by giving her the secret to his strength. Each time, Samson lied to her and gave her a fake source of his gift. On each occasion, Delilah delivered the message to the Philistines. They, in turn, tried to attack Samson with that supposed weakness, but the Philistines died instead.

Despite knowing her intentions, Samson maintained his relationship with Delilah and stayed in the Kill Zone, both physically and spiritually! Eventually he gave in and told her the power of not cutting his hair. Delilah passed the secret along and the Philistines used this knowledge to capture Samson.

Samson was bound and taken to trial. During Samson's trial, his hands were tied to the front two pillars of the courthouse. Before Samson was put to death, he called out to God for strength and forgiveness. God heard Samson and granted him his last earthly request by giving Samson one last bolt of energy. Samson used the strength to push the two pillars apart, causing the entire building to collapse on the Philistines and himself, killing all within the walls.

I find this story to be painful as I read about Delilah's attempts to find Samson's weakness. Her persistence and his willingness to remain in the Kill Zone of temptation led to his eventual demise.

Practical Exercise

1. Why did Samson continue his relationship with Delilah?

2. What is one possible reason Delilah was assisting the Philistines?

3. List those in your life who are helping you.

4. Who are the people in your life who are hurting you? How?

THE DELILAH CYCLE

"Adolescence can be understood as a unique opportunity in which the changes taking place in the brain affect the individual throughout his or her entire adult life."
-Dr. Jennifer Brown

Why do we do this to ourselves? Why do we keep going back to our Delilah even though we know it hurts us? There are two main reasons this happens.

First, your body is created to maintain what is known as homeostasis. Your body regulates hot and cold temperatures through the natural processes of sweating, goose bumps, blood flow, digestion, etc. This same principle is true for the mind. While studying the behavior of soldiers and police officers, clinical psychologist Kevin Gilmartin[2] discovered that the brain does the exact same thing. Through research and studies, Gilmartin discovered that the brain has a natural process to ensure that our moods and emotions stay within a range of homeostasis by not going too high or too low. Our minds like to be at ease!

Our brain has a toolbox of hormones, neurotransmitters, steroids, and a host of other chemicals that help ensure the mind stays within homeostasis. Mental homeostasis is a range of emotions within boundaries that the mind has set. It is a range rather than an exact spot (see the Delilah Cycle Graph for reference). If you are slightly sad or happy, the brain allows time to alter your mood. However, if you have a severe feeling of sadness, then your brain kicks into work and starts releasing specific chemicals—which we are going to call "happy" chemicals—to bring your mood back within the homeostasis boundaries. The opposite is true, too. If you get overly excited, your brain helps bring itself back down to acceptable levels with "calm" chemicals.

Now bring in Delilah, who represents whatever our personal temptation may be. She makes us feel good both physically and mentally. As we think about and anticipate our Delilah, we begin to boost our emotional state. After building up the anticipation, we finally climax and have a euphoric release after Delilah has been consumed. This circumstance is what we call instant gratification. It is a quick build up with a euphoric high after very little work or effort. The result? A major dump of feel-good chemicals (like dopamine) into our system.[3]

Do the words *euphoric* and *high* sound like the mind is at ease? Absolutely not! The "high" causes our mind to be out of the homeostasis range. So, naturally, our brain freaks out. "Oh, no! Something is wrong! We had better fix this before we hurt ourselves!" The brain releases the "calm" chemicals to bring our mind's emotional state back down.

To help you understand the next section, I would like to give an example from the physical world. Have you ever been bowling with your family using the bumper lanes? I loved using the bumper lanes as a child because it kept the ball on the lane instead of in the gutter. I would push the ball down the lane and it would slowly bounce from one side to the next until it reached its destination. Keep that image in your mind as we read this next section.

What happens to us immediately after a sin is committed? I can tell you exactly how I feel after committing a serious sin. The euphoria quickly subsides and the mixed emotions of guilt, shame, realization, hopelessness, anger, and frustration are felt. These feelings are like spraying cold water on your mind, and it causes a literal physical and emotional drop! This results in an emotional plummet below our homeostasis line. Now we have a chemical, physical, and emotional depression, or what I call a triple threat, to use a phrase from my basketball days.

*Disclaimer: This level of depression may not be noticeable at first. You will most likely start by rationalizing your actions. Nevertheless, as the sinning continues, the guilt builds and leads us to this cycle.

We do NOT like to be depressed. Our mind wants to be at ease, right? No one wants to stay sad. Our mind responds by trying to find ways to make us happy again, but we keep hashing over our sin and don't allow our mind to work its way back up. This is straight from Satan's playbook. He reminds us of the sin, he tells us God does not want a sinner, he tells us how worthless we are, and he tells us how embarrassed we will be if others find out about it. He does everything he can to keep us from naturally getting back to homeostasis.

Then Satan reminds us of Delilah. "You know what, we felt really good when Delilah was around!" Now we begin the anticipation and expectation of feeling good again. We start climbing up the dark stairwell trying to get back to homeostasis.

Then we consume our Delilah. Whether it is physical, mental, visual, or chemical doesn't matter! All that matters to us and to Satan is that we consume it. Now we are feeling good, but there's a problem. We don't feel AS good as last time because we had a lower starting point. But it does feel good and we bask in the dopamine dump that got us here, even if it only lasts a moment. Then the guilt and shame reappear, and we crash even lower than before! We are lower because we had a lower peak than last time. The Delilah Cycle Graph on the next page gives you a visual representation of this process.

This cycle repeats itself over and over again as you can see in the graph. This is where our natural man really kicks in. Instead of stopping the cycle and getting off this roller coaster, we decide to increase our time with Delilah. More drugs, more alcohol, more egregious pornography, more food, more social media, more music, or whatever our sin of choice may be. This allows us to have a higher high again. But we cannot escape the cycle from within the cycle. What I mean is this: You cannot end the cycle while participating in it. You will continue having lower highs and lower lows. From within the cycle, the only way to combat the decline is with an increase of use.

The Delilah Cycle is one reason that people stay in the Kill Zone, but I want to tell you that we can completely avoid the cycle! We do not have to suffer and go through this. By knowing what it is and what it looks like, we can avoid it. If you are already in the cycle, there is hope! I promise you that as you continue reading this book, you will find your answers for escape. Keep going!

The Kill Zone • 27

Delilah Cycle Graph

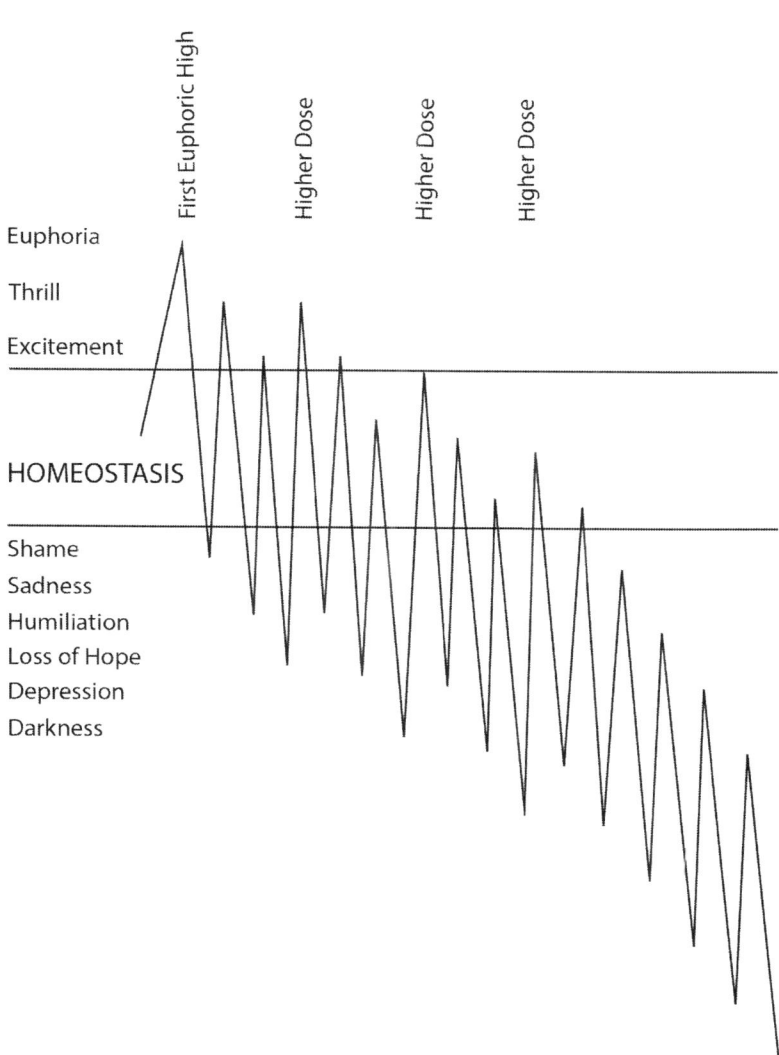

In addition to the Delilah Cycle, there is a second reason we stay in the Kill Zone. As a police officer, I found myself asking these questions every day: Why in the world would this person or that person make those incredibly dumb choices? Why would that father or mother give up their family for drugs? Why would that teacher risk his job and livelihood for pornography? I was so bothered by this that I began to ask, *"Why? Why would you risk it all for this?"*

And I got my answer: Flash Bang!

Practical Exercise

1. Where do you see the Delilah Cycle in your life? How is it impacting your happiness?

2. Who do you see going through this cycle? What are they doing?

3. The number one step toward recovery is recognizing the problem. Be honest and write your Delilah below. Ask your parents to share their personal Delilah's as well. Name them, recognize them, and next I will teach you how to defeat them!

FLASH BANG

A flash bang is a handheld device used by military and police forces. The design is similar to a hand grenade. It has a pin that you pull out, and then you release the hand lever which starts a countdown. Unlike a hand grenade which explodes to kill people, the flash bang is not designed to kill. Instead, it is designed to disorient people inside a home or room. This allows the police to enter the room with little to no resistance. To accomplish this, the device does three things. First, a magnificent flash of light bursts from the device and causes temporary blindness. Second, an ear-bursting "bang" causes your ears to either burst or feel like they are going to. Third, the burst of noise causes a literal sound wave that fills the room with its vibrations. The flash, bang, and wave cause your mind and body to be overwhelmed. The mind simply cannot compute everything that is happening to it, so it shuts down and focuses only on itself.

Now I am going to turn Delilah into a flash bang. Satan throws the flash bang into your life via negative or impure thoughts, ideas, media, friends, electronics, and so forth. When the flash bang enters your life, you have a few short seconds to respond to it. You can cover your ears and close your eyes, run to the next room, kick it out of the room, or just wait and see what happens.

When we wait to see what happens, the flash bang goes off, causing immediate blindness and disorientation. You can only focus on how you feel at that exact moment - no thinking of the future and no remembering the past.

When we allow a temptation or sin to linger, it's like a flash bang going off in the brain. Satan blinds us to the consequences of our actions. We become focused on how we feel at that exact moment, and we don't consider what we have been taught or the consequences that will follow. Satan did everything he could to keep King David's focus on Bathsheba and the pleasure of the sin. Samson focused on Delilah, Cain focused on pride, Judah focused on a harlot, Judas focused on money, and the list goes on and on. Satan does not want you to see what will happen WHEN your sin is discovered. He doesn't let you see the pain you will cause yourself and others. If he did, how many of us would chase after Delilah? If we saw how much it hurts, we wouldn't do it! If we saw the faces of our parents and loved ones and remembered the lessons they taught us, we wouldn't give in to temptation. If we thought about the discussion with our future spouse telling them of our addictions and seeing the look of disappointment in their eyes, we would flee the situation.

A flash bang is meant to cause us to freeze so we cannot leave or fight back. If you come across pornography, music, impure memories, excessive self-doubt, or other random mental temptations, these are examples of flash bangs. They have been placed in your mental path to consume your focus. If you allow them to stay, then they keep you in the Kill Zone. Instead of freezing, kick those suckers out of the room before they have time to go off!

Quick Tip

The process to fortify your mind, soul, and body from Satan's temptations is discussed below. However, I want to share a tip that can make HUGE improvements right now! During my own fight with pornography, I discovered a way to immediately cast Satan from my mind. We know that light and darkness cannot occupy the same space, which is true for the mind as well. By shining light in your mind, the temptation is immediately expelled. What does this light look like? The next time you have one of those thoughts enter your mind, think to yourself, "It's not over until the fat lady sings!" Then sing your favorite song that has a positive and uplifting message. Whether it is in your mind or vocally, sing loud so that it fills your mind and allows no space for Satan and his minions!

I personally use songs from my church primary class days. Children's songs are easy to remember and have powerful lyrics and catchy tunes, which make them perfect for our use. I have added two songs at the end of the book to help you start. When you sing these songs, just keep repeating them until the negative thoughts have been dispelled. Immediately say a prayer after the thoughts are gone, asking God for help to keep your mind clear. If the thoughts return, then just keep singing. Obviously, the more songs you remember, the easier this will be. Over the years I have found four songs that I use. I chose the songs because of the calming tunes and empowering words. I suggest you stay away from songs with complex arrangements. Pick songs that are meaningful and anchored to your spiritual core. Songs from your church, family, or community group are great sources.

BATTLEFIELDS

In life we must meet new people, attend social events, and use electronics, cell phones, and social media. Likewise, exercise, education, dating, marriage, and work are but a few examples of different things we must do in life to be successful and find meaning. These are normal activities that are expected and required to advance our way of life.

Let me ask you this: Are any of these things inherently wrong? Are cell phones bad? Is dating bad? Are TV, work, electronics, media, etc.... bad?

We can agree that these things are not inherently bad. In fact, they are gifts from God that can be used to accomplish incredible feats. You and I can do SO much good in these areas! I would venture a guess that your church uses these things for the work of God. Doesn't your church, community group, and family ask you to date, post on social media, work hard, be healthy, and watch uplifting TV and videos? We even use these things in our Sunday classes.

If we know that these things are a necessary part of life, don't you think Satan knows that, too? Don't you think it's possible that he uses these opportunities to attack your soul and the souls of our fellow brothers and sisters?

The following two scenarios are 100% true. Even though they are difficult subjects, they highlight how Satan turns every day circumstances into battlefields.

Tactical Scenario 1

I would like to introduce you to my one and only uncle, CJ. What does CJ stand for? I don't know. What is he like? I don't know. You see, when he was in his twenties, he wanted to expand his group of friends to those that looked more fun. He wanted to be at the weekend bonfires with the loud music, alcohol, and nice cars that he kept hearing about. He started attending parties and socializing with individuals who were making bad choices. He began dating girls who had NO desire to be married, let alone attend any house of religion. These actions quickly led CJ to the use of illicit drugs, inappropriate relationships, and many addictions.

Late one night, Uncle CJ had a fight with his drug dealer over a girl and drugs. The argument ended when my uncle murdered his drug dealer. He was caught, convicted, and sent to prison where he spent over 25 years in confinement.

Practical Exercise

1. What initial actions did CJ take that eventually led to murder?

2. What were his consequences?

3. What actions do you see in your life that can lead to more detrimental situations if they are not stopped or addressed?

Tactical Scenario 2

While sitting at home reading after putting my children to bed, my wife called me in a complete panic. She was away attending a game night with close friends. The party was disrupted with a loud knock at the door where two police officers awaited a response. When our friend and owner of the home answered, the two police officers explained to her that they had arrested her husband. They informed her that her husband was sitting in the back of the patrol car awaiting the drive to jail and that creating child pornography was the charge. I was a police officer at the time, and my wife asked that I come down and find out what was happening. She also asked me to help explain things to our stunned friend! Questions of how to take care of their four children and soon-to-be-born baby were high on the list of concerns.

In the following months, it was discovered that her husband had been using his time alone to view pornography. Using his phone and computers, he became addicted to pornography and the feelings it created. However, as we have discussed earlier, these feelings became less powerful with each use. He needed more and more exposure to feel the same high. Eventually, he had to act on the things he watched to create the same high as before. As he tried to create the high he desired, the pornography-related actions increased until he was finally discovered by the police.

His actions led to the loss of his career, financial strain on his family, and time away from his children while he was in jail.

Side note: Through God's love and forgiveness, this wonderful man has changed. He now enjoys life with his patient and loving wife and children. He did not allow the sin or Satan to define him. Instead, he has created a program to help men who suffer from addictions to find recovery, hope, and help!

Practical Exercise

1. Why did he have a desire for more pornography?

2. Who was hurt by his actions?

3. What can you do to protect yourself from similar circumstances?

Let's circle back and remember that Satan views EVERYTHING we do as a potential battlefield. Dating is not bad unless you date exclusively before you should. Playing sports is wonderful unless it takes over your life and stops you from doing what God expects you to do. Social media is good unless you obsess over it or use it for inappropriate purposes. Music is amazing unless you use it to numb your soul and spirit. Sleeping is necessary, but sleeping 12 hours every day will stunt your progression. Sex is incredible and natural unless you prematurely or disrespectfully wield its power.

Everything in life can be used for good or bad. Your job is to ensure that you are using it for good. You must intentionally make choices and act rather than be acted upon. To do this, you will need to be properly equipped with your armor for the battle. Before we describe your armor, though, let's discuss the question: "Can you withstand Satan's temptations?" Honestly, the answer is no – not if you stay in the Kill Zone!

STAY ALERT, STAY ALIVE!

"Now I beseech you, brethren, mark them which cause divisions and offences contrary to the doctrine which ye have learned; and avoid them." -Romans 16:17-20

"Complacency: A feeling of contentment or self-satisfaction, especially when coupled with an unawareness of danger, trouble, or controversy." -TheFreeDictionary.com

Let's jump back to me kicking in the door of the Mellow Yellow trailer. What do you suppose I was feeling before, during, and after I kicked in the door? Words like euphoric, excited, adrenaline dump, and natural high come to mind. I didn't have a care in the world! Do you know what else happened? Nothing, absolutely nothing. I walked through that house without a tactical thought in my mind, and nothing bad happened to me. In fact, no one was even home! I just walked into that house with all good feelings and there was not one repercussion for my less-than-tactical entry.

Tactically speaking, when I walked through that door, was I in or out of the Kill Zone? Think of the movies you have seen. When the door gets kicked in or even blown open, do the officers just waltz in? Or do they come in running "hot and heavy?" With my entry, did I leave myself open to being shot?

When we attend that party, when we view those images, when we go on single dates, when we stay up late into the morning on our phones and tablets, at first it's euphoric! Nothing happens to us. Sure, alarm bells are going off in our head and telling us that we are exposing ourselves to trouble. But what evidence is there? Nothing bad happened, so we continue these actions and even increase their frequency. What could possibly go wrong?

Ramadi, Iraq - December 24th, 2005: My team and I were searching for Improvised Explosive Devices (IEDs/bombs) along the main supply routes in the Sunni Triangle. Our assignment was to clear the roadways of IEDs, terrorists, and any other person or thing meant to harm U.S. and Allied soldiers. I remember when we had first begun our mission months before. It was the biggest adrenaline dump I have ever had in my life, and I suspect nothing will ever come close again!

Each day was potentially my last. By December we had driven the routes hundreds of times and I had had close encounters with death on a regular basis. But even then, the "Oh, my goodness, I almost died" feelings just weren't that high anymore. Despite all the close calls on our patrol, our team had never been harmed, which led to our adrenaline rushes subsiding. It also led to us letting our guard down by not being alert like we were when we started.

On this fine Christmas Eve day, we were driving on the same dirt road that we had driven every day for months without harm or incident. The road only had one way in or out. We knew that, and our enemies knew it, too. The entrance to this road was the perfect example of a Kill Zone.

I guided my Humvee onto the dirt road by driving off the paved highway. My front tires dropped off the pavement as I slowly rolled forward. I eased on until my back tires dropped off the pavement and then - complete darkness!

Slowly the darkness started to subside. It went from black to dark brown, then to light brown. At first it was completely silent, then the sound slowly increased until it reached an incredibly high-pitched ringing! The sights, smells, and sounds mixed with yelling will never be forgotten. The most memorable thing is the metallic and gun powder taste - a taste that comes flooding back every time I go target shooting.

The explosion destroyed the rear end of our vehicle, rendering it undrivable. We became sitting ducks to any potential attacks from enemy soldiers. Luckily, Heavenly Father protected us as we sustained only minor injuries, and no one attacked us as we recovered the vehicle.

If you attend that party, view those images, go on single dates, or stay up late into the night on your phones and tablets, you may not have an issue at first. Like our time in the Humvee, it starts with good feelings and no repercussions. But like the explosion on Christmas Eve, you will also have a spiritual explosion if you allow yourself to stay in the Kill Zone!

While attending Officer Candidate Training for the Army, a seasoned drill sergeant conveyed the following story to my training group. This story has been a great reminder in my life about the dangers of complacency.

During the African campaign of World War II, a British Special Forces battalion was marching across the hot desert. They hung their heads from severe exhaustion brought on by the fighting and the hot sun that blazed down on their worn bodies. As they marched, a second and equally exhausted Special Forces group marching in the same direction slowly integrated into the British ranks.

After several hours of marching, a member of the second group tripped on a rock, causing him to fall to the ground. The fall resulted in him yelling out in pain and frustration–in perfect German. The two sides realized they were marching not with allies but with enemies and immediately engaged in combat. The battle that ensued between the surprised and tired German and British Special Forces soldiers was one of the bloodiest recorded in World War II history.

Like the soldiers in both of these stories, we find ourselves waking up and simply going through the motions. Instead of staying away from potential battlefields, we enter them with little thought of protecting ourselves. When we become complacent and let our guard down, we give the enemy an opportunity to break through our nonexistent defenses!

Ask yourself whether or not you are driving your soul through the Kill Zone on purpose. Have you become indifferent to the dangerous consequences that can result from your decisions? I assure you that Satan and his followers are analyzing your movements, appetites, desires, hopes, dreams, habits, and actions. Satan has placed spiritual bombs in your path, just like those enemy soldiers set the bomb for me to drive over. He is waiting for you to become complacent to the dangers of where you spend your time and thoughts and for you to recklessly navigate your spirit through the Kill Zone so that he can then destroy your soul!

Can you withstand Satan's temptations? It depends. If you allow yourself to enter Satan's battlefield, then SATAN WINS. As they say in gambling, "The house always wins." Just like a casino cheats you out of your money, Satan will cheat you out of your soul. If you play on Satan's battlefield, then you will lose. That is the point of this entire book: DO NOT PLAY ON SATAN'S FIELD! God is a creator; he has created a field for you to play on. It's called God's Zone of Light, and we'll talk more about it later. Go there, and don't stay where Satan can hurt you. Instead, go where God has set you up for success.

You must become fully aware of your weaknesses. You know your own heart and your own weaknesses, and Satan knows them, too. Think about it - this means that you know where Satan is going to attack! Make every effort to stay away from those situations. Mark Twain said it best: "It is easier to stay out than to get out!" Know thyself and protect thyself!

Spend a moment and list five potential Kill Zones that Satan may try to exploit in your life. Need help getting started? I wrote my five as an example. Ask your parents to share theirs with you as well.

Justin's List
1. Anger
2. Pride
3. Fear
4. Pornography
5. Substance Abuse

Your List
1.
2.
3.
4.
5.

Your Parent's List
1.
2.
3.
4.
5.

ACE

In the beginning of the 2003 Iraq War, the United States Government came up with an ingenious idea to help soldiers remember the names and faces of enemy fighters. They issued playing cards with the enemies' faces on them and gave the cards to the soldiers. That way, as the soldiers played cards, they would see the faces and names to help them remember. The value of the card corresponded with the value of the target. The faces on the 2 cards were the lowest targets, and the Ace cards were the highest targets.

The world is full of temptations and threats that Satan can throw at us - well over the 52 playing cards used by our military forces. In the last chapter, you identified your personal top five Kill Zones that Satan will likely use or is currently using against you. Think of these as your personal Ace cards. Be mindful of them and be sure to take extra precautions when it comes to your thoughts and feelings in these areas.

As I reflect on my time as a police officer and look at the world we live in today, I have no doubt that Satan's Ace card for our modern times - and the number one threat to youth and adults - is pornography! In this chapter, we will discuss recent history, current threats, the lie, the facts, and then future development. This is a tough subject that we must tackle! Do not shy away from this topic.

The threat is real. The danger lies inside your home, in your pocket, and in your hand. After reading this chapter, I implore you to sit down with your parents and create a safety plan. As a son or daughter, wouldn't you like to help set the terms?

Please know that gone are the days of parents and youth speaking to each other in passive tones or code words. Satan and his followers are working hard for your soul. It is time to be bold and speak about pornography head on!

What is Pornography?

The first thing we have to do is define what pornography is because you may not realize how much it encompasses. Dr. Jill Manning, an expert on the subject, defines pornography like this: "Pornography is material specifically designed to arouse sexual feelings in people by depicting nudity, sexual behavior, or any type of sexual information. This can refer to pictures, stories, sounds, symbols, actions, or words that depict bodies and/or sexual behavior. Pornography can also be created, distributed, and consumed using any type of media. For example, television, radio, books, film, photographs, magazines, cartoons, drawings, videos, DVDs, CDs, telephones, cell phones, iPods, video games, websites, webcams, and live performances (such as strip clubs) are all ways pornography can be distributed and consumed."[4]

That is a long list! You have to understand that pornography can come in many forms. The main thing to remember is that it's something that causes you to feel sexually excited. Sometimes that can happen with images or videos, but it can also happen with books or magazine articles. Men and boys are usually drawn to visual forms of pornography, while women and girls are often more affected by explicit stories because of the emotions associated with reading that kind of material. Males and females are different, but both genders can be affected by pornography.

Sometimes you will come across pornography that may not be sexually exciting, but it still gives you an uncomfortable feeling inside. Pay attention to those feelings! That is your warning from God that what you are viewing, reading, or listening to isn't appropriate and that you are entering Satan's battlefield if you linger. Drop what you're doing and get out of the Kill Zone!

If you are old enough to read this, there is a high probability that you have already been exposed to pornography. The first encounter with pornography often happens around eight years old. By age 12, the majority of youth have been exposed to one degree or another.

You MUST have sensitive but anatomically correct conversations with your parents. Body parts need to be identified and the general idea of the amazing process of sex described. Do not wait to ask questions! Give your parents the opportunity to be the first ones explaining the process, sacredness, and purpose with you. Let your parents know that these subjects are not difficult! They are plain and beautiful. Let them know that you don't want to be ashamed of or hidden from the truth. This chapter will help lay out the steps for you to have these conversations with your parents. As you both read this book, you will have the opportunity to teach your parents and be taught by them. You will have the opportunity to discuss many things, including the natural process of sex, which was given to us by God to be used as an expression of commitment, love, oneness, and creation.

Please keep in mind that not long ago, these conversations oftentimes did not occur in homes. Parents were taught that the mere suggestion of sex, drugs, and other addictive behaviors put the ideas in their children's minds. The truth is that the ideas and images are already there. In fact, they have always been there. You are going through the same changes, feelings, chemical fluctuations, thoughts, ideas, and desires your parents and your grandparents experienced at the same age. You are already experiencing sexual feelings physically, spiritually, and mentally, correct? That is because the process is natural and created by God. Discussions of these changes and how they all fit into a beautiful plan of love and marriage are vital. This all starts right here, right now with bold and open conversations. The goal is to keep these discussions going... FOREVER!

History of Pornography

The threat of pornography has not always been Satan's Ace card. It has grown into what we see today in a relatively short amount of time. In fact, in my lifetime I have watched it go from a 5 of Clubs with limited exposure to Satan's Ace card!

I grew up in a small town in southeastern Utah. I lived in the middle of the desert about ten miles from civilization. Our TV antenna only brought four channels into the home, so most of my time was spent outdoors playing.

Somewhere between the ages of 8 and 10 years old, I was introduced to pornography by my friends. As the years went by, computers became more prevalent and so did access to pornography. I continued to view pornography with the help of certain friends until a computer was placed in my own home. As the ability to see pornography continued to increase, so did my appetite for it. My friends and I grew up in a time where parents were not ready to combat the growing tide of pornography. Children were being taught computers in school while parents had to learn on their own.

Churches, organizations, and family groups were also unprepared for the explosive access and the addictive nature of pornography. As a youth, my knowledge and ability far exceeded that of my parents and leaders. Then came the experts on TV and radio proclaiming that pornography was good for parents, adults, and children. We were told that pornography helped children learn in their developmental years, that it helped marriages stay strong, and that it was the cure for all sexual transgressions.

The easier access and the ever-increasing confusion of pornography's harmful consequences led to the inability of parents, churches, and other organizations to effectively fight the industry and keep their children safe. I am a product of the confusion and misinformation. It is only because of my wife, my education, and the Atonement of Jesus Christ that I escaped the vicious cycle with the steps that I will teach you.

Modern Threat

Times are changing and the negative effects of pornography have been documented. The destruction to families is obvious. We now know that pornography is not good for us. We now know that it is not good for marriages. Pornography leads to pain, divorce, and an increase in sinful behavior. We see it happening right before our eyes. I grew up in the middle of the digital porn wave. I have watched more friends than I can count ruin their lives with this plague! What started as a youthful curiosity was carried into adulthood and has destroyed marriages, separated families, and ruined careers.

Today the pornography industry has infiltrated every home through smart phones, smart TVs, and other smart devices. In fewer than five seconds, an individual can access the very worst things Satan has to offer!

History of the Lie

This battle is reminiscent of the fight against tobacco. Before the 1960's, tobacco was advertised as healthy. Doctors, government workers, and experts all proclaimed smoking as a healthy habit. Then came the scientific proof of the dangers of tobacco use. It was proven that tobacco companies paid doctors, government workers, and experts to lie to the public.

Now we see it again. The pornography industry has doctors, psychiatrists, therapists, and experts who freely lie for them. As the truth of pornography's avoidable consequences continues to come out, the requirement to fight this industry increases. It is now known that pornography damages our brains, families, sex drive, physical health, and our soul.[5] Just like smoking, we cannot use the excuse that we don't know how bad it is!

Winning Strategy

So, how do we win? Does it require us to give up all electronics? Absolutely not. It starts with three easy steps: You must speak to your parents openly, truthfully, and frequently.

Openly: Ensure that you have an open line of communication with your parents. This requires patience and love in your communication with them. Your parents were raised to not think, say, or do anything regarding sex... EVER! Many parents felt and still feel guilty or embarrassed about sex due to the way they were raised, so when you start having these conversations, be aware that your parents may be uncomfortable at first. Be prepared to show love and understanding of their feelings. Empathy is your number one tool. Over time, your conversations will help build confidence in each of you. This will blossom into a long-term relationship of open conversations that will bless you throughout your life.

With this openness, you need to express the feelings you have about electronics. You must also express your weaknesses. Your parents will communicate why they are concerned and what your family will do about it. I have advised them to be open and not sneak around. No buying salt shakers that block signals to phones. No messing with the cell phone plan. Instead, have open communication on how, when, where, and why the electronics will be used. Also, allow open inspection of the phones. You should be able to inspect your parents' phones and they inspect yours! Remember that you and your parents are on the same side, and that is the side against Satan. Be mindful and respectful of the agreement.

Open communication about sex will begin. Your family must use the proper terms for the body. Penis, vagina, breasts, and buttocks are body parts just like feet, head, hands, and armpits. (Ew, armpits!) In your parents' book, there are instructions for them to approach you and begin a discussion on sex. No matter your age or what you know, you must have this conversation with your parents! They will guide you and answer any questions you may have, and they will be completely open and truthful in their responses.

Truthfully: Again, use proper terms when you have these discussions. It doesn't matter how uncomfortable you feel using those words. The more uncomfortable it is, the more important it is that these discussions happen! As you have these conversations, the words will become easier to use over time.

You must be truthful with yourself and your parents and know that pornography <u>will</u> be seen, even if it's through no fault of your own. Remember, the first exposure for children happens on average around eight years old, and most youth have seen pornography by the age of twelve. This is a fact, this is truth, and you must be prepared for it! Do not lie to yourself and think, "It won't happen to me." Do not lie to your parents or act like you are not seeing pornography! It happens, so be honest and let them know so they can help you find ways to limit the exposure.

Remember that what you see on TV, in the media, and on the internet is not real sex. It is fake and will create a false sense of reality. It is extremely important that you learn the true nature of what sex REALLY is and why God created it. I am not talking about the 8-year-old discussion on the birds and bees. I am speaking about the deep and personal discussions of the body, emotional preparation, roles of husband and wife, and the art of being selfless and devoted to your spouse.

In traditional Jewish culture, the parents are responsible to teach their children how to properly please their future spouse. In their culture, honorable parents teach their children how to become men and women by focusing on the pleasure of their spouse. This concept completely escapes Hollywood's interpretation. Instead, Hollywood focuses on selfishness and the demeaning of women.

Your parents will teach you the truth. They will set you up for success and a higher sense of pleasure and satisfaction in your future marriage and love life!

Frequently: This is not a one-and-done conversation. This process must be nurtured and continued. At the very least, this needs to be a monthly conversation. I suggest setting a weekly time that you can have a one-on-one conversation with your parents. Put it on your schedule and let nothing get in its way! This is where you can discuss pornography, proper use of phones and computers, school, friends, goals, problems, successes, and how to react **when** exposed to pornography.

Help your parents establish boundaries with your use of electronics. No one should have a personal electronic device by themselves, not even your parents! A good practice is to turn in your phone each night. Ask your parents to set the example by also doing this. I have found the kitchen to be a great place, as it has plenty of plugs and is central to the home. Remind your parents that they are not immune to Satan's temptations just because they are adults.

Establish a NO ELECTRONICS day or evening with your parents. Breakfast, lunch, and dinner should be a time for your family to discuss things without any distractions. This goes for prayer and scripture time as well. Turn the electronics in and turn them off. The temptation to look at the phone if a text pings is too powerful.

Studies show that a notification from the phone releases a small dose of dopamine, which gives you a jolt of excitement. Do you ever get a text during class or church and you literally feel a pull to look at it? Try this out: next time a text comes in, see how long you can go without looking at it or without thinking about it. That pull and desire to look is your brain seeking that drop of dopamine. In other words, you're addicted to it!

Turning your phone off for 15 minutes during breakfast and lunch and 30 minutes at dinner equals one hour. Take the 1 hour and add 30 minutes for family scripture study and prayer and that's only 1.5 hours a day. I promise the world can get by without you for that 1.5 hours, but your family can't! You need that time to learn and grow from your discussions. You need to set the standard that families are more important than any post on social media. This time spent together is a great opportunity to have those open, truthful, and frequent conversations.

Let's wrap this chapter up. Satan is no respecter of persons. He will not pass by you or your parents without trying to drag you down. I must warn you, the more you take the action steps listed above, the more ambitious Satan will be to harm you! However, the more action steps you take, the less power he will have to harm you. I promise that each temptation you hurdle over will make the next one even easier. Over time, instead of hurdles, they will simply be pebbles to walk over.

"But, Justin," you may say, "I text every night until 2 or 3 in the morning, and I have never looked at porn!" First of all, I don't believe you. Second, porn is not the only temptation or problem that could arise. Think about and write here what other threats Satan may pose against you on your phone:

_____

_____

_____

_____

_____

_____

Here is the Truth

"Your son is looking at porn," I replied. My friend responded in horror and shock, "No he isn't!" He had just finished telling me that he allows his children to keep their phones 24/7, including in their rooms at night. I challenged him to go home and speak with his son about his phone use. He accepted my challenge with an "I'll show you" look.

A few days later, I received a call from the same friend who said, "Let's meet for lunch." He had a sound in his voice that was urgent and unbending. I agreed and met with him an hour later. As soon as we sat down, he dove into his story. After our conversation he told me that he could not shake the feeling that he needed to speak with his son concerning pornography. He went home that first night and pushed off the feeling to speak with him. He went to work the next day and the feeling would not leave his mind. After dinner he went to his son's room where his son was sitting on the bed playing with his phone. My friend sat down next to him and simply asked, "Is there anything you would like to tell me?"

His son stared at him for a few minutes in silence, and then broke down. "I have been looking at porn on my phone," he said. During their discussion, it was discovered that a habit had been formed and it had been going on for an extended amount of time. My friend looked at me and said, "Thank you." We then spent the rest of the meal discussing how other parents can protect their children from the same fate.

This is what I call cyber warfare! Here is the truth: **your phone is the single greatest threat to your well-being**. It is proven that it lowers your self-esteem, causes depression, increases bullying, and leads to a lower level of mental health.

Please, go through the Suggested Action Steps at the end of this book. Help your parents establish clear, concise, and reasonable ways to protect you and your family.

Pornography Facts

Let's go over the known facts for a moment:

1. There are no studies that show a benefit to using pornography.[6]
2. According to a study done by the Barna Group, 79% of men ages 18-30 view porn at least once a month. 63% of men in that age group view porn at least several times a week.[7]
3. The same study reports that 76% of women ages 18-30 say that they view porn at least once a month.[8]
4. The clinical practice of Dr. Mary Anne Layden has proven that pornography damages the sexual performance of those who view it.[9]
5. Brigham Young University (BYU), a private religious college, did a study of students nationwide that found:[10]
    a. 48% of male students reported viewing pornography at least weekly.

b. 86% of male students had viewed pornography in the last year.
   c. 1 in 5 male students view pornography daily or nearly every day.
6. There are dozens of studies linking the use of pornography to an increase in depression, anxiety, and poor cognitive function.[11]
7. There is overwhelming evidence that porn use leads to poor relationships.[12]
8. Over 28% of the workforce in the United States spends 2-3 hours a month looking at porn, resulting in BILLIONS of dollars in lost revenue.[13]
9. The average age of first exposure keeps dropping with studies now showing that it occurs between 8-11 years old.[14]
10. It is the most-searched topic on the internet.[15]
11. It destroys families.
12. It kills the soul.
13. It ruins lives!

Future Development

I wish I could tell you that the threat will go away in the future. I wish I could express a hope that the industry will implode and disappear, but I can't. Instead, I must issue a dire warning.

The industry has only begun. The development in robots, neurotransmission, and brain uploading and downloading are things from sci-fi movies that have become reality. The tip of the commercialization of these products is already happening throughout the world.

We are also seeing a shift in audience targeting. Like big tobacco, they have begun their campaigns on younger children and women. All they see is the money that they can make in these industries. That is why we are seeing the age of first exposure drop to 8 years old and young adult women now viewing at a rate of 75%. That is the porn industry's new target!

By now, I hope you have a clear picture of what the pornography industry is doing. I hope you see that they are targeting you! So, how do you keep from getting struck by Satan's arrows? How do you gain the strength and abilities to get out of the Kill Zone? How do you have the strength to say no? How do you have the strength to turn your head and close your eyes?

BATTLE ARMOR

"Put on the whole armour of God, that ye may be able to stand against the wiles of the devil." -Ephesians 6:11

"Be sober, be vigilant; because your adversary the devil, as a roaring lion, walketh about seeking whom he may devour; Whom resist stedfast in the faith" -1 Peter 5:8-9

Each day Satan spends every second doing everything in his power to draw us into the Kill Zone. He is not limited by physical strength, time, sleep, hunger or thirst. He is limited by one thing and one thing only! (What is he limited by? Find the answer below). This means that each day we must wake up with the intention to do battle. Just like a police officer or a firefighter or a soldier in a war zone would never perform their jobs without proper protection, neither should you.

I would like to introduce you to my good friend, Joseph. You may know him by the coat of many colors that was stolen from him. Most people who read about him look at his life and say, "Wow, he had a lot of trials!" One such trial is when he ended up as a slave in the household of Potiphar. Potiphar was a powerful man in the land of Egypt under Pharaoh's rule. Through Joseph's hard work and dedication, Potiphar became impressed with Joseph and soon gave him command of all his household.

Do you remember what happened next? It can be assumed that Joseph's rise to power as a servant and his apparent good looks brought him the attention of many people. One such person was Potiphar's wife. Potiphar's wife soon started to ask Joseph to commit a serious sin with her. She desired him to "lay with her," which in modern terms means she wanted to have sex with him. Let's be honest - if Joseph had allowed his mind to remain in the Kill Zone, he could have created some powerful rationalizations on why it was okay to commit the sin. For example:

1. Potiphar's wife wielded power. If he remained in her favor, she could have convinced her husband to release Joseph and send him home.
2. Giving in would have brought ease to his life as she would have given him even more favor in the home.
3. No one would have found out. She would not have admitted it because the offense would have meant death for her as well.
4. God had seemingly abandoned him! Here he was in Egypt as a slave where he could have questioned if God even existed or cared about him.

So here is Potiphar's wife tempting him day in and day out. She keeps harassing the poor kid. One day she takes a hold of his jacket and continues to tempt him. What does Joseph do? Let's look at Genesis 39:8-9.

"But he refused, and said unto his master's wife, Behold, my master wotteth not what is with me in the house, and he hath committed all that he hath to my hand;

"There is none greater in this house than I; neither hath he kept back anything from me but thee, because thou art his wife: how then can I do this great wickedness, and sin against God?"

If we took the first three words and put them into action in our daily life, we would be completely fine! **"But he refused!"** Underline that, mark it, color it like the rainbow. That is the key! He didn't ponder, he didn't wonder, he didn't question and debate. He didn't research it on his tablet – (did you see what I did there?)

He REFUSED!

After refusing, Joseph told Potiphar's wife that he respected his master (her husband), and he reiterated his code of honor. What did he do next? He followed the advice given by prophets of old. 2 Timothy 2:22 says, *"Flee also youthful lusts: but follow righteousness, faith, charity, peace, with them that call on the Lord out of a pure heart."* Joseph saw that flash bang and ran away!

By reading the account of Joseph and Potiphar's wife, we know Potiphar's wife had been bothering him for a while. Joseph woke up every day prepared to do battle with Satan (who was working through Potiphar's wife). He had his answer ready. He was ready for the Kill Zone! 1 Corinthians 16:13 explains where Joseph stood: *"Watch ye, stand fast in the faith, quit you like men, be strong."*

Are you ready to suit up like Joseph of old? Joseph may not have worn physical armor, but by golly, that man had one incredible suit of spiritual armor!

Helmet

Matthew 9:4 states, *"And Jesus knowing their thoughts said, Wherefore think ye evil in your hearts?"* First, we will start where Satan starts: the mind! We must protect our thoughts and desires by putting on our spiritual helmet. How do you put on your spiritual helmet? You simply have a desire to do good! We are promised that this desire acts like a tiny mustard seed of hope, and a desire to follow God will grow into a powerful movement in our mind and soul. Mark 4:20 says: *"And these are they which are sown on good ground; such as hear the word, and receive it, and bring forth fruit, some thirtyfold, some sixty, and some an hundred."* A hundredfold! Talk about a return on your investment.

Hebrews 12:2-3 explains that we should fix our eyes upon Christ. He is the one who suffered and died for us, so He has the power and ability to help. We are promised that, with His help, we will not grow weary and we will have the mental strength to focus on our Savior. We must think of Christ, believe in Christ, and hope in Christ. The more we do this, the more strength will flow into our minds.

Sword

Next is our sword. Psalms 119:11 explains, *"Thy word have I hid [treasured] in mine heart, that I might not sin against thee."* The word of God is the sword! We cannot fight effectively without our sword, so feast upon the words of God. Hebrews 4:12 says, *"For the word of God is quick, and powerful, and sharper than any two-edged sword, piercing even to the dividing asunder of soul and spirit, and of the joints and marrow, and is a discerner of the thoughts and intents of the heart."* The word of God is your most powerful tool!

Tell me this: When you watch movies where swords are used, isn't it fun to watch the swordplay? Of course it is! There is a reason that movies of flashy swordsmen are still being made. It's exciting, it's fun, and you almost can't get enough of it. This must be our attitude toward our scriptures. Imagine while reading them that you are literally in a sword fight with Satan. Use the scripture masters around you, and with this sword you will cut through Satan's lies and temptations. You will win when you feast on the word of God!

How does reading the scriptures give you power over Satan? *"And the Lord spake unto Moses face to face, as a man speaketh unto his friend"* (Exodus 33:11). The scriptures are God's way to communicate with you in physical form. Use them if you're needing answers to your questions and concerns. Use them if you need guidance in a decision. Use them if you need support or strength at a difficult time. Dig into the scriptures and He will use his direct phone line to answer. Crack them open--God is on the other end!

Shield

Now we move on to the shield. Oh, the shield. When Spartans fought, they had a very distinct order of the importance of their weapons. First came the spear, which they would jab, throw, and sweep. Do you know what the second weapon of offense was? You guessed it – the shield. With the shield, the Spartans would push, smash, cut, and destroy the enemy that stood before them. The shield was thought higher than the Xiphos (a short, broad sword) that they kept on their hip.

Your shield is prayer, which you can use to push Satan away, smash his plans, cut open his lies, and destroy his wicked designs! Let your hopes, concerns, problems, and solutions be known to God. Prayer is your greatest defense and can be your greatest offense. Prayer will bring peace to your heart. It will allow you to share your struggles with God. It will also help you manage those struggles with an eternal perspective!

I want you to think of a time that prayer has protected you. If you can't think of one or doubt its protection, let me show you that you are just not seeing it yet.

When I was young, I went through a time in my life that I could not see God's answers to my prayers. However, eventually I took the time to look back and find his hand in my life. Here are a couple of experiences.

While driving home late one night from a basketball game with a car full of friends, I fell asleep at the wheel. The car began to drift off the road toward a large embankment. As clear as if I was standing next to a blaring foghorn, I heard a friend yell, "Justin!" I awoke, corrected, and checked which friend I had to thank for keeping us alive. You guessed it, everyone was still asleep. I thought to myself, "Wow, someone in this car must be special to be protected by God."

I already told you how I was driving a Humvee when I drove over an IED and shrapnel spewed throughout the interior of the vehicle but didn't strike any of us. I remember looking at my buddies that were in the Humvee and thinking, "Wow, I keep spending time with amazing people who are protected!"

While sitting on a bridge in Iraq, my gunner leaned over his gunner's hatch to spit out some sunflower seeds. When he looked over the edge, he discovered that we were sitting only six feet away from a ginormous bomb! Enemy soldiers had placed it there to kill us. We quickly got away and later discovered that the bomb builder had forgotten to turn on the triggering device. Guess what my thought was: "Holy moly, that gunner sure was protected!"

After a while, I think God was getting frustrated with my lack of vision. One day, after almost dying from a near miss with a boulder, I had a very clear "Aha" moment. I realized that maybe, just maybe, I was the one being protected. You will also have that moment--please don't take as long as I did, though! Take time to ponder and remember the blessings in your life, even the smallest ones!

Battle Buddies

In Proverbs 27:17 we read, *"Iron sharpeneth iron, so a man sharpeneth the countenance of his friend."* In the military we call this the battle buddy system. It is a serious offense if you are caught without your battle buddy. He or she is there to support you and watch your back no matter where you go. This system has proven extremely effective in the military. It keeps you safe and protected by having an extra brain and set of hands and eyes with which to work and make decisions.

While in high school, I made strong relationships with fellow Christians of other faiths and we spent all our time together. Other students in the school (unbeknownst to our group until graduation) called the hallway we hung out in the "Jesus Corner." They meant it as an insult, but I have worn that distinction with pride. After all, as Matthew 18:20 says, *"For where two or three are gathered together in my name, there am I in the midst of them."*

During this time, I recognized the power of battle buddies. We kept each other accountable and filled our time with wholesome activities. Changing my circle of friends allowed me to have more of God's light in my life and set me on the path to overcoming my pornography addiction. I recognized a direct link between my successes or failures and those I surrounded myself with, and this is important for you to understand, too. Who you spend your time with matters! When you hang out with losers, you do loser things.

As we read Exodus and the many difficulties with the Israelites leaving Egypt, I can only imagine how frustrated Moses was. It seems like every problem became a huge trial for the people, which Moses had to guide them through. This was exhausting for Moses. Finally, he received an answer in Exodus 18:22. Moses was counseled to select judges who were charged with hearing the concerns and griefs of the people and dealing with them. The judges were given this duty to "bear the burden" with Moses.

I encourage you to find your battle buddies and hold each other accountable. In James 5:16 we are counseled, *"Confess your faults one to another, and pray one for another, that ye may be healed. The effectual fervent prayer of a righteous man availeth much."*

Ask your friends, and expect to be asked by them:

1. Did you pray today?
2. What did you read in the scriptures?
3. What victories have you had today?
4. Where can I help?
5. You aren't going out with her/him by yourself, are you?
6. Going for a drive? Great! We would all love to join you!

I will forever be in all my friends' debt as they guided me through the hiccups of life. I promise that as you find and develop these friendships, you will be blessed beyond measure. Their love, acceptance, and strength will carry you throughout your life!

Ultimate Warrior

"There hath no temptation taken you but such as is common to man: but God is faithful, who will not suffer you to be tempted above that ye are able; but will with the temptation also make a way to escape, that ye may be able to bear it."
-1 Corinthians 10:13

To become the Ultimate Warrior, you must take the three main lessons taught in this book and apply them to your life. First, read your scriptures, pray, and protect your thoughts by putting on a spiritual helmet. Second, you must create a family support network by applying the advice we spoke of in the chapter on family. Third, create a network of friends that will support you along the journey as we discussed in the last section. When you apply all three of these action steps, you will become an Ultimate Warrior. You will wake up each day prepared for war by doing your duties with faith that God will take care of you.

In Luke 8, a city official approaches Christ and begs him to bring his daughter back to life. Jesus follows the man home and, in an intimate setting, raises the girl from the dead. What did he do after that—do you remember? Jesus recognizes that she is hungry, and he commands those around him to get something for her to eat. Jesus had just raised her from the dead. How easy would it have been for him to just fill her belly with food? Loaves and fishes, anyone? But he didn't; he told those around him to do it. Why would he do that? The answer is simple.

God takes care of the impossible. He leaves the possible to us – to you!

During the loaves and fishes miracle, Jesus required the apostles to search for all the food they could find amongst the people. After collecting the loaves and fishes, he then performed the miracle. He required the preparation of the wine barrels before he performed the miracle of turning the water into wine. Jesus even required the father of the little girl to escort him to the father's home before he would raise her from the dead. God is ready to perform miracles in your life, but you must be willing to take the first steps. I challenge you to do the possible!

As a daughter or son of God, you have accepted the challenge to do the possible. This includes reading scriptures, praying, attending worship, developing your family, choosing good friends, keeping away from tempting situations, and being in the right place at the right time to maintain a tactical advantage over Satan.

One more thought. When you think of a warrior's physical appearance, what do you see? I'm going to add one more category. It is health. You have been entrusted with a temple of flesh and bone. As you respect it and take care of it, God will bless you with increased mental and physical strength. I am not saying that you have to look like a Spartan, but you must do your best at taking care of the temple you have been entrusted with.

As you follow this plan, you will become an Ultimate Warrior!

Practical Exercise

1. What are the three action steps?

2. Sit down with your family and schedule a time that you can read and pray every day together.

3. Which piece of armor do you need to work on most? Write a goal and commit to doing just a little better on it - starting now!

4. What does your family need to work on?

5. Which one of your friends can you help do better?

The Creed

A creed is a set of beliefs which guide your actions. It is a way to declare what you believe and what you will do with those beliefs. By declaring your creed, you will motivate yourself and give courage to those you are with.

Turn to the last page of the book to find a cut out of the Ultimate Warrior Creed. Post it where you can see it often and read the creed out loud each morning and evening.

You may be asking yourself, *Do I really need to read it out loud?* The answer is yes! Let me explain. Each one of us has something called a subconscious, which controls what our body and mind do automatically. Reading the creed twice a day will help it to become part of your subconscious. It will help those principles become automatic in your life. Remember that the creed is your declaration of what you believe and how you will act on those beliefs. If you are like me, though, you are not perfect at each declaration. You may struggle with reading your scriptures and praying every day. Maybe you are afraid of speaking boldly to others. These are just habits that have not been built yet, but they can be built! It is as easy as reading the creed every day and doing your best to live by it. It will take time, but it will happen, and it will be worth the effort.

Take courage in the fact that thousands of other girls, boys, young men and young women are also declaring the creed every morning and night. Refer to it with your personal battle buddies and, as a community of Ultimate Warriors, we will lead others out of Satan's Kill Zone!

Ultimate Warrior Creed

I am the Ultimate Warrior.

I am a disciple of Christ.

I honor God by living the commandments.

I speak truth with boldness.

I am physically and mentally disciplined.

I diligently seek knowledge by studying my scriptures.

I stand ready to recognize, evade, and conquer my enemy, Satan.

I am a guardian of freedom and the Christian way of life.

I prepare daily with my helmet, shield and sword.

I never accept defeat.

I never quit.

I am the Ultimate Warrior.

Your Source of Power

After Jesus fasted for 40 days, he was met by Satan, who tempted him three times. After fending off Satan twice, Jesus was taken to the top of the Temple Mount and told by Satan to jump off the top of the temple to prove that he would be protected by angels. How did Jesus respond to Satan's temptation? Go to Luke 4:12 and look at the first three words: And Jesus answered.

And - Right away and without delay

Jesus - Came straight from him; no angels or disciples delivered the message

Answered - No debate or thought; it was immediate, personal, and decisive

Let that resonate in your mind and think of the power this response had on Satan. Do you think he had any doubt in Jesus's stance or position? Did he question who was more powerful? Did he fear Jesus and his ability to withstand him?

Now comes the knowledge of Satan's limited power. Here Satan had his mortal and spiritual enemy standing on top of the Temple Mount. I have a question for you: Why didn't Satan push Jesus off the temple to kill his mortal body? After all, without Jesus Christ, we would be lost in our sins to Satan's grasp and Satan would be left to rule and reign!

The truth is that Satan couldn't behave in that way because he is limited! Satan cannot cross certain lines because he is limited in power and scope by Jesus Christ. Jesus was sent to earth by God to complete the Atonement. God, having the ultimate power, gave his son, Jesus Christ, that ultimate power and authority. This example alone proves it.

As a daughter or son of God here on earth with a mortal body, you have been given the authority to rule over the creatures of the earth. Genesis 1:26 says, *"Let us make man in our image, after our likeness: and let them have dominion over the fish of the sea, and over the fowl of the air, and over the cattle, and over all the earth, and over every creeping thing that creepeth upon the earth."* Did you see how God specifically mentions "every creeping thing that creepeth upon the earth?"

Even though Satan looks like you and me, in what form did Satan first introduce himself to Adam and Eve? A SERPENT! So, who has the ultimate power and authority? YOU do! Genesis 1:27 says, *"So God created man in his own image, in the image of God created he him; male and female created he them."* You are created by

God to resemble Him and are thereby given power to rule over the creatures on earth!

The only power Satan has is the power we give him. He can mentally tempt us by encouraging thoughts and feelings, but that's it! Any influence he has beyond this line is strictly by our permission only.

I pray you find hope and power in this fact! If you are not giving YOUR power to Satan to influence your actions, then you will remain safe. In other words, if you are not lingering in the Kill Zone, then Satan has NO POWER over you.

Allow the power of this knowledge to strengthen your mind and spirit!

God's Zone of Light

"And he said, My presence shall go with thee, and I will give thee rest." -Exodus 33:14

Interestingly, God created the original concept behind the Kill Zone. But like all good things, Satan takes that which is good and twists it to use for his evil designs. It began as God's Zone of Light. God knew that the more we keep him in our mind and heart, the easier it is for us to do good. Satan took that lesson and realized that keeping a person in darkness decreases light and decreases the ability to resist sin.

While you are in the presence of God, *"Ye are the light of the world"* (Matthew 5:14). There are two options to choose from. First, Satan's ultimate plan is to bind you in sin so that he can drag you down to hell! How does he do that? He uses the Delilah Cycle we spoke of before. Once you sin, he does everything he can do to make you feel ashamed of your sin, which pushes you into the cycle. Once there, your mind seeks to hide itself in darkness and self-pity. The farther you go into the darkness, the less light (and help) you will see. The truth of the matter is this: *"No man can serve two masters: for either he will **hate the one, and love the*** *other;* *or else he will hold to the one, and despise the other. Ye cannot serve God and mammon" (Matthew 6:24).*

The second option is to follow God. God wants you to be free from sin and bask in his light. When you follow God, he sets you upon the hilltop to be a light (or a beacon) to all those around you. This light comes from your knowledge of and trust in God. It is the faith that he will be with you every step of the way.

What do you do to stay in God's Zone of Light? You wear your armor of God. Feast upon the words of God. Stay close to God by listening, praying, thinking about him, and pondering on his words. Allow God the time to fill you with as much light as possible!

1 John 4:16 says, *"And we have known and believed the love that God hath to us. God is love; and he that dwelleth in love dwelleth in God, and God in him."* The apostle had an "Aha" moment and shared it with us in this scripture. When we dwell in love, we dwell with God. The result is that God dwells in us because we are dwelling in love, and "God is love." Love and be loved!

When we show more love, it will result in more of God's love poured on us! Now here is the neat part: Do you remember Delilah's cycle for homeostasis? Can you recall the general decline as shame entered our life and how we marched down the scale of depression, shame, and self-pity? This process of love is how we march our way back up the scale! Can you imagine that? You do not have to be stuck in the cycle of pain. You do not have to accept your current location in life. Instead, through God's love, he will literally lift you back up the scale toward homeostasis and keep you there!

The Promise to Cain

I remember when I first spoke to my religious leader about pornography and the effects it was having on my life. He was loving and helpful throughout the process of repentance. I remember him sitting in his chair with love and concern in his eyes. He leaned forward, looked me straight in the eyes and said, "Justin, the Lord has forgiven you of these sins. The most difficult thing you will face is forgiving yourself."

That discussion happened over 20 years ago. We still speak today, and I view him to be a close friend and mentor. I consider him a pivotal influence in my life. What he told me has been 100% correct! After that repentance process, I was buried in guilt. By allowing the guilt to consume my mind, I gave in to Satan's temptations for my Delilah. It took me another ten years of hard-fought battles to finally learn how to get the upper hand! At age 25, I finally learned who has the real power: ME! However, this is an ongoing process. I am not saying that I am now free from Satan's temptations. Still to this day, he tries to push me back into shame.

If you are caught up in the whirlwind of sin and shame, I am here to throw you God's lifeline! God loves you, he needs you, and he stands ready to pull you out of the Kill Zone! It took me 25 years to learn the lessons you have been taught here. I echo my mentor's counsel: The most difficult part of getting away from your Delilah is the shame and guilt you feel about it! As explained before, this is Satan's tool for power. When we allow doubt to linger in our mind, we give him permission to control us.

Here are some stories that are great examples of God's love! Trust me—if these individuals can be blessed by God after their sins, then so can you!

Let's start with the very first murderer on earth, Cain. Have you ever read past the part about him killing his brother? First, in Genesis 4:11-12, God curses Cain for the slaying of Abel: *"And now art thou cursed from the earth, which hath opened her mouth to receive thy brother's blood from thy hand. When thou tillest the ground, it shall not henceforth yield unto thee her strength; a fugitive and a vagabond shalt thou be in the earth."*

Ouch! That is a harsh punishment! I am sure Cain had lost hope and was full of shame for his actions. He pled with God: *"And Cain said unto the LORD, My punishment is greater than I can bear. Behold, thou hast driven me out this day from the face of the earth; and from thy face shall I be hid; and I shall be a fugitive and a vagabond in the earth; and it shall come to pass, that every one that findeth me shall slay me"* (Genesis 4:13-14).

Be honest, do you feel badly for Cain right now? He just murdered his brother and now he is complaining about having to wander in the wilderness and work. Luckily for Cain, we are not the ones deciding his fate. God responds, *"And the LORD said unto him,*

Therefore whosoever slayeth Cain, vengeance shall be taken on him sevenfold. And the LORD set a mark upon Cain, lest any finding him should kill him. And Cain went out from the presence of the LORD, and dwelt in the land of Nod, on the east of Eden" (Genesis 4:15-16).

Sevenfold? God would punish anyone that kills Cain sevenfold?! That's right; that was his promise. You are reading this book, and I highly doubt the sin you are struggling with includes murder. God loves Cain, and he loves you! He wants to do everything he can to help you return to him. Considering how he felt about Cain who committed the most serious sin, just imagine the blessings he holds for you!

Do you remember David's eventual fate? His actions caused the death of Uriah and over 70,000 Israelites! After David's repentance, God said that King David was a man after his own heart. God allowed King David to remain king, which led to his son Solomon's rule. Again, I don't know your sin, but I have a hard time believing that it also led to 70,000 deaths! God still forgave David and kept his covenant with him. God WILL forgive you. Start marching forward!

The greatest lessons Jesus taught were told in story form. The same goes for the wonderful lesson of forgiveness. The story of the prodigal son is a beautiful story of love wherein the prodigal son took his inheritance and wasted it on frivolous purchases and sinful living. When the money ran out and all was lost, the prodigal son returned home with the hope of just being a servant in his father's household. His father, however, received him with open arms and even threw a party to celebrate his son's return.

Jesus Christ paid for your sins. If you have wandered from His presence, please know that He awaits your return to the fold with arms wide open. Take the lifeline and return to bask in His love and protection. Within His arms we find true happiness!

Conclusion

You have been taught what the Kill Zone is, you have been taught that you should avoid it, and you have been given the tools and armor that will help you make the decision to get out of the Kill Zone when the time comes.

I testify to you that if you take the six steps—communicate openly and effectively with your parents, look to God, read his word, pray, know your weaknesses, and surround yourself with good friends—then you will recognize the Kill Zones in your life. I promise this will strengthen you for the battles that lie ahead. You can live in confidence that you will be victorious!

Suggested Action Steps

1. With your parents, create boundaries for electronics use in your home. Use those boundaries to write a family safety plan for electronics. Post it in each bedroom and in a common room.
2. Designate a turn-in location for phones and tablets.
3. Schedule weekly personal interviews with your parents.
4. Create a schedule for personal and family prayer, scripture study, and devotionals. Use the simple checklist in the back of this book to track your progress and keep yourself and your family accountable.

Songs

Remember that light and darkness cannot occupy the same space. When Satan tries to trap you in the Kill Zone, positive and uplifting music is an excellent way to get out of the darkness and back into the light! The following two songs have helped me many times to do this.

Onward, Christian Soldiers

Onward, Christian soldiers, marching as to war,
 With the cross of Jesus going on before.
Christ, the royal Master, leads against the foe;
 Forward into battle, see his banners go!

Onward, Christian soldiers, marching as to war,
 With the cross of Jesus going on before.

At the sign of triumph Satan's host doth flee;
On, then, Christian soldiers, on to victory.
Hell's foundations quiver at the shout of praise;
Brothers, lift your voices, loud your anthems raise.

Like a mighty army moves the church of God;
Brothers, we are treading where the Saints have trod.
 We are not divided; all one body we:
 One in hope and doctrine, one in charity.

Onward, then, ye people; join our happy throng.
Blend with ours your voices in the triumph song:
 Glory, laud, and honor unto Christ, the King.
This through countless ages men and angels sing.

Text: Sabine Baring-Gould
Music: Arthur S. Sullivan

Called to Serve

Called to serve Him, heav'nly King of glory,
Chosen e'er to witness for his name,
Far and wide we tell the Father's story,
Far and wide his love proclaim.

Onward, ever onward, as we glory in his name;
Onward, ever onward, as we glory in his name;
Forward, pressing forward, as a triumph song we sing.
God our strength will be; press forward ever,
Called to serve our King.

Called to know the richness of his blessing--
Sons and daughters, children of a King--
Glad of heart, his holy name confessing,
Praises unto him we bring.

Onward, ever onward, as we glory in his name;
Onward, ever onward, as we glory in his name;
Forward, pressing forward, as a triumph song we sing.
God our strength will be; press forward ever,
Called to serve our King.

Text: Grace Gordon, alt.
Music: Adam Geibel, 1855-1933

About the Author

Justin Zufelt has lived a life of service to his family, his community, and his country. He joined the Army in 2001 and was deployed to Iraq in 2005. He was awarded the Purple Heart after sustaining injuries when his Humvee drove over an IED. Justin now serves as an Army Officer in the Chaplain Corps and helps other soldiers and families overcome the challenges of military service. One way he accomplishes this is through teaching Strong Bonds marriage classes to soldiers and their spouses.

Justin is no stranger to spiritual and emotional battles. As a youth, he struggled with an addiction to pornography and has also dealt with the effects of PTSD after combat service. He now brings a wealth of knowledge from his experience as a distinguished war veteran, military officer, police officer, SWAT team member, federal law enforcement officer, business owner, and recovering addict. His desire, mission, and goal is to help others create a purposeful and fulfilling life!

Justin is the founder of Operation Onward Miracle, which is helping youth discover their inner spiritual strength as they navigate a world plagued by pornography. He is also the co-founder of Wealth Mentality Families, which teaches families to pursue true wealth.

Justin and his wife, Leilani, are the parents of five beautiful children. Their family loves to travel together, and their most recent adventure included an RV expedition through Mexico.

BIBLIOGRAPHY

[1] Webster, Teri. *TheBlaze*. 9/2/2018. https://www.theblaze.com/news/2018/09/02/us-russia-nix-formal-united-nations-discussions-on-so-called-killer-robots

[2] Gilmartin, Dr. Kevin. *Emotional Survival for Law Enforcement*. (Tucson: E-S Press, 2002).

[3] Horvath, Tom. "How Does Addiction Affect the Brain?" *MentalHelp.Net*. 2016. https://www.mentalhelp.net/articles/how-does-addiction-affect-the-brain/

[4] Manning, Dr. Jill C. *What's the Big Deal about Pornography*. (Ann Arbor: Sheridan Books, 2008), 2-3.

[5] Layden, Dr. Mary Anne. "U.S. Senate Hearing on the Brain Science Behind Pornography Addiction and the Effects of Addiction on Families and Communities." 11/18/2004. http://www.drjudithreisman.com/archives/Senate-Testimony-20041118.pdf

[6] Gungor, Mark. *Laugh Your Way to a Better Marriage*. (New York: Atria Paperback, 2008), 191.

[7] CovenantEyes. *Porn Stats (2018 Edition)*, 8. www.covenanteyes.com/pornstats/

[8] Ibid.

[9] Gungor, Mark. *Laugh Your Way to a Better Marriage*. (New York: Atria Paperback, 2008), 191.

[10] Hadfield, Joe. *BYU News*. 12/7/2007. https://news.byu.edu/news/byu-study-college-women-more-accepting-pornography-their-fathers

[11] "Studies linking porn use to poorer mental-emotional health & poorer cognitive outcomes." https://www.yourbrainonporn.com/relevant-research-and-articles-about-the-studies/porn-use-sex-addiction-studies/studies-linking-porn-use-to-poorer-mental-emotional-health-poorer-cognitive-outcomes/

[12] "How Porn Hurts a Consumer's Partner." *Fight the New Drug*. 8/23/2017. https://fightthenewdrug.org/how-porn-hurts-a-consumers-partner/

[13] "Internet Pornography by the Numbers; A Significant Threat to Society." https://www.webroot.com/us/en/resources/tips-articles/internet-pornography-by-the-numbers

[14] "What's the average age of a kids first porn exposure?" *Fight the New Drug*. 7/30/2018. https://fightthenewdrug.org/real-average-age-of-first-exposure/

[15] "Top 100 Most Searched Topics on the Internet." *Seattle Organic SEO*. 1/29/2015. https://seattleorganicseo.com/top-100-searched-topics-internet/

Personal	Helmet	Shield	Sword	Physical Activity
Sunday				
Monday				
Tuesday				
Wednesday				
Thursday				
Friday				
Saturday				

Personal	Helmet	Shield	Sword	Physical Activity
Sunday				
Monday				
Tuesday				
Wednesday				
Thursday				
Friday				
Saturday				

Personal	Helmet	Shield	Sword	Physical Activity
Sunday				
Monday				
Tuesday				
Wednesday				
Thursday				
Friday				
Saturday				

Personal	Helmet			Shield			Sword			Physical Activity		
Sunday												
Monday												
Tuesday												
Wednesday												
Thursday												
Friday												
Saturday												

Personal	Helmet			Shield			Sword			Physical Activity		
Sunday												
Monday												
Tuesday												
Wednesday												
Thursday												
Friday												
Saturday												

Personal	Helmet			Shield			Sword			Physical Activity		
Sunday												
Monday												
Tuesday												
Wednesday												
Thursday												
Friday												
Saturday												

Family	Helmet	Shield	Sword	Devotional
Sunday				
Monday				
Tuesday				
Wednesday				
Thursday				
Friday				
Saturday				

Family	Helmet	Shield	Sword	Devotional
Sunday				
Monday				
Tuesday				
Wednesday				
Thursday				
Friday				
Saturday				

Family	Helmet	Shield	Sword	Devotional
Sunday				
Monday				
Tuesday				
Wednesday				
Thursday				
Friday				
Saturday				

Family	Helmet				Shield				Sword				Devotional			
Sunday																
Monday																
Tuesday																
Wednesday																
Thursday																
Friday																
Saturday																

Family	Helmet				Shield				Sword				Devotional			
Sunday																
Monday																
Tuesday																
Wednesday																
Thursday																
Friday																
Saturday																

Family	Helmet				Shield				Sword				Devotional			
Sunday																
Monday																
Tuesday																
Wednesday																
Thursday																
Friday																
Saturday																

Ultimate Warrior Creed

I am the Ultimate Warrior.

I am a disciple of Christ.

I honor God by living the commandments.

I speak truth with boldness.

I am physically and mentally disciplined.

I diligently seek knowledge by studying my scriptures.

I stand ready to recognize, evade, and conquer my enemy, Satan.

I am a guardian of freedom and the Christian way of life.

I prepare daily with my helmet, shield and sword.

I never accept defeat.

I never quit.

I am the Ultimate Warrior.

Made in the USA
Columbia, SC
24 April 2019